Switzerland's Hidden Gems

Discovering Distinctive Tourism Destinations

Ronnie Sedlak

Table of content

Introduction

Welcome Message

Hello and welcome to "Switzerland's Hidden Gems: Discovering Distinctive Tourism Destinations." Your ticket to discovering Switzerland's lesser-known yet breathtakingly gorgeous locations is this handbook. This book will reveal the gems that are hidden away from the well-traveled routes, whether you are an experienced tourist or are organizing your first trip.

Introduction to Switzerland's Diverse Landscape and Culture

Switzerland is a remarkably diverse nation. Its scenery is as varied as it is stunning, ranging from the majestic Alps' highest peaks to tranquil lakes and charming villages. With influences from nearby France, Germany, and Italy, the Swiss culture offers a distinctive fusion of customs, tongues, and delectable cuisine. Switzerland's diverse regions each have their own unique appeal, creating a patchwork of scenic beauty and cultural diversity.

Purpose and Scope of the Guide

This guide's objective is to introduce you to Switzerland's hidden treasures, which are sometimes overlooked in favor of the country's more well-known tourist attractions. The goal of this book is to give comprehensive information on these unusual places, covering their background, main draws, and helpful travel advice. We hope that by discovering these hidden gems, we will improve your trip and encourage you to take advantage of everything that Switzerland has to offer.

Overview of Switzerland's Geography

Each of the areas that make up Switzerland has distinct geographical and cultural traits. The country's east and south are dominated by the majestic Alps, which are an outdoor lover's dream come true. While the northern section combines urban sophistication and rural peacefulness, the middle region is known for its rolling hills, immaculate lakes, and quaint towns. With its French influence, the western region is home to picturesque vineyards and ancient cities.

Brief Introduction to the Regions Covered in the Book

This guide covers a range of regions, each with unique hidden gems:

- **The Enchanting Alps**: Zermatt, Saas-Fee, Lauterbrunnen Valley, and Aletsch Glacier.
- **Hidden Lakes and Waterways**: Lake Oeschinen, Caumasee, and Lake Brienz.
- **Charming Towns and Villages**: Appenzell, Gruyères, and Murten.
- **Cultural and Historical Treasures**: The Abbey of Saint Gall, Bellinzona's Castles, and Romainmôtier Priory.
- **Natural Wonders**: The Creux du Van, Emosson Dam and Dinosaur Tracks, and the Rhine Falls.
- **Off the Beaten Path**: Val Mustair, the Bregaglia Valley, and the Lavaux Vineyards.
- **Adventure and Outdoor Activities**: Via Ferrata routes, paragliding in Interlaken, and winter sports in Engelberg.
- **Relaxation and Wellness**: Thermal baths in Leukerbad, Bad Ragaz, and the Emmental region.

Unique Geographical Features

Some of Europe's most remarkable natural features can be found in Switzerland's diverse geographic regions. Highlights include the Alps, where peaks like the Matterhorn provide famous views. In addition, the nation is home to a number of immaculate lakes, including Lake Geneva and Lake Lucerne, as well as distinctive geological formations, including the Creux du Van. There are countless chances for exploration and adventure because of this diversity.

Importance of Exploring Hidden Gems

While seeing well-known sites like the Matterhorn and Lake Geneva is a must, discovering hidden jewels will give you a more personal and distinctive view of Switzerland. These lesser-known locations provide an opportunity to experience the local way of life, take in the pristine natural beauty, and get away from the throng. They also offer a greater comprehension of the varied topography and lengthy history of the nation.

Benefits of Discovering Lesser-Known Destinations

Exploring lesser-known locations can significantly enhance your vacation experience. These locations frequently provide more genuine interactions with regional customs and ways of life. You can take advantage of more sedate, less commercialized settings and discover unusual sites that are not commonly known to tourists. Furthermore, visiting these locations promotes sustainable tourism practices and boosts the local economy.

Enhancing the Travel Experience

Going off the beaten road will allow you to experience Switzerland as it truly is. Experiences that will stick with you include hiking through undiscovered paths in the Alps, relaxing by a remote lake, and touring quaint towns that haven't been overrun by tourists. With any luck, this guide will provide you with all the knowledge you need to maximize your travel experiences and make sure that every place you visit will have a lasting impact.

Explore the unmatched beauty and cultural diversity that lie beyond the well-known landmarks as you go on this journey through Switzerland's hidden gems.

Map of Switzerland

Chapter One: The Enchanting Alps

Zermatt and the Matterhorn

Tucked down behind the recognizable Matterhorn, Zermatt is a charming village that perfectly captures the allure and magnificence of the Swiss Alps. Zermatt is a paradise for nature lovers and outdoor enthusiasts, known for its lively atmosphere, historic wooden chalets, and car-free streets.

Overview of Zermatt Village

Zermatt village offers a beautiful fusion of contemporary conveniences with old world charm. Its cobblestone streets provide a variety of quaint cafes, fine dining establishments, and boutique stores for tourists to peruse. The Matterhorn Museum offers an intriguing look into the heritage of the area and the mountaineers who have tried to summit the imposing peak. The community is rich in history.

Zermatt Village

Zermatt

Hiking and Skiing Opportunities

Outdoor enthusiasts can enjoy year-round activities in Zermatt. It becomes a skier's paradise in the winter with more than 200 kilometers of slopes that are appropriate for all ability levels. With guaranteed snowfall, the resort also has one of Europe's highest ski areas. The scenery opens out in the summer to expose a system of hiking trails suitable for both novice and expert hikers. At 3,089 meters, the Gornergrat Railway, a cogwheel train, offers breathtaking vistas and access to a multitude of hiking pathways.

The Iconic Matterhorn

Due to its pyramidal shape, the Matterhorn is perhaps the most famous peak in Switzerland and serves as a symbol of the Swiss Alps. With its elevation of 4,478 meters, it draws climbers from all over the world. The Matterhorn Glacier Paradise, Europe's highest cable car station, provides panoramic views of the surrounding peaks and glaciers for those who aren't inclined to approach its heights.

Matterhorn Switzerland

Saas-Fee: The Pearl of the Alps

Situated in an elevated valley and encircled by thirteen peaks surpassing 4,000 meters in elevation, Saas-Fee is commonly known as the "Pearl of the Alps." With its rustic architecture and welcoming ambiance, this quaint community provides a true alpine experience.

Winter Sports and Summer Activities

Saas-Fee is a top winter sports destination with 150 kilometers of slopes and a solid snowfall record. With its top-notch terrain parks, snowboarding and freestyle skiing are its main draws. With routes leading to stunning vistas and alpine cottages, the area becomes a refuge for hikers and climbers in the summer.

Saas-Fee

Saas-Fee Ski Resort

Glacier Experience

The world's tallest subterranean funicular connects you to the Allalin Glacier, which offers year-round skiing and snowboarding. Visitors can explore the ice innards and learn about glaciology at the intriguing exhibition area called the Ice Pavilion, which is carved out of the glacier.

Local Culture and Traditions

With annual traditional festivals and activities, Saas-Fee manages to preserve a strong feeling of its unique culture. The community is renowned for its colorful folklore, which includes the procession of painted cattle through the streets during the Alpine descent of the cows.

Lauterbrunnen Valley

With its verdant meadows, towering cliffs, and tumbling waterfalls, Lauterbrunnen Valley is frequently referred to as one of the most picturesque valleys on Earth. The valley provides a tranquil getaway into nature and serves as an entrance to the Jungfrau region.

Waterfalls and Scenic Beauty

There are seventy-two waterfalls in the valley; the most well-known being Staubbach Falls, which plummets about 300 meters from an overhanging rock wall. Another must-see is the Trümmelbach Falls, a set of underground cascades that demonstrate the unadulterated power of glacial meltwater and are reachable by a tunnel lift.

Staubbach Falls

Trümmelbach Falls

Hiking Trails and Adventure Sports

The Lauterbrunnen Valley has a vast network of hiking trails suitable for all skill levels, ranging from easy strolls through meadows full with flowers to strenuous climbs through the mountains. With options for base jumping, rock climbing, and paragliding, adventure sports are also quite well-liked.

Local Folklore and History

The valley's allure is enhanced by its rich folklore and history. Fairies and mountain spirits are mentioned in local traditions, and the classic chalets and barns showcase architectural styles that date back hundreds of years. The alpine farming customs and cultural legacy of the valley are revealed at the Talmuseum Lauterbrunnen.

Talmuseum Lauterbrunnen

Aletsch Glacier

The largest glacier in the Alps and a UNESCO World Heritage site is the Aletsch Glacier. This 23-kilometer-long natural wonder offers a breathtaking ice and snow panorama.

Aletsch Glacier

UNESCO World Heritage Site

Recognized for its exceptional natural beauty and ecological value, the Aletsch Glacier is a part of the Jungfrau-Aletsch Protected Area. For scientists conducting study, especially in the domains of glaciology and climate change, the region serves as a living laboratory.

Guided Tours and Hiking Tips

For those who want to have a closer look at the glacier, guided tours offer secure entry to its vast frozen surface as well as knowledgeable explanations of its movements and development. Hiking routes in the vicinity provide the opportunity to explore the high alpine environment and breathtaking views of the glacier.

Environmental Significance

Scientists can gather important information on climate change from the Aletsch Glacier's receding ice sheet. Visitors are urged to abide by rules in order to reduce their influence, as efforts to preserve this delicate ecosystem are extremely important.

Set out on an incredible adventure through the Enchanting Alps, where new discoveries await around every corner and every stop offers a distinctive experience. The Swiss Alps are a treasure trove of undiscovered jewels, from the famous Matterhorn and the quaint town of Zermatt to the pure beauty of the Aletsch Glacier.

Chapter Two: Hidden Lakes and Waterways

Some of Switzerland's most charming and lesser-known attractions are its immaculate lakes and serene canals. This chapter covers some of the lesser-known aquatic treasures that provide unmatched scenic views, a wide range of activities, and tranquil settings ideal for both leisure and exploration.

Lake Oeschinen

Activities and Attractions

Lake Oeschinen, a breathtaking alpine lake renowned for its pristine blue waters and spectacular mountain backdrop, lies tucked away above the town of Kandersteg. Popular outdoor pursuits around the lake include hiking, fishing, rowing, and, in the winter, ice skating. A unique and enjoyable way to take in the beautiful scenery is to go on a toboggan run along the lake during the summer.

Scenic Beauty and Relaxation Spots

The serene surroundings of the lake offer plenty of places to unwind and have a picnic. The meadows and wooded areas around the property are ideal for relaxing and soaking in the breath-blowing views. For those looking for a quiet getaway in the great outdoors, Lake Oeschinen is a great choice because of its beautiful surroundings and glistening pure water.

Access and Transportation

From Kandersteg, Lake Oeschinen can be readily reached by gondola ride, short trek, or electric shuttle bus. A wonderful trip is ensured by the breathtaking views of the valley and mountains that come with the gondola ride.

Lake Oeschinen

Caumasee: The Turquoise Jewel

Best Times to Visit

Caumasee, in the Flims area, is renowned for its vivid turquoise waters, which are especially vivid in the summer. The months of June through September are ideal for visiting because of the pleasant weather and the lake's peak beauty.

Swimming and Boating Activities

Caumasee is a well-liked location for boating and swimming. There are several wooden pontoons on the lake that are great for diving and tanning. You may hire rowboats and stand-up paddleboards so that guests can take their time exploring the lake.

Surrounding Flora and Fauna

Lush woodlands encircle the lake, offering a home to a wide range of animals. Experience the local flora and creatures in their natural habitat by going on nature walks and going birdwatching in this ideal location.

Caumasee

Lake Brienz

Boat Tours and Water Sports

The Bernese Oberland's Lake Brienz is well-known for its crystal-clear blue waters and breathtaking mountain vistas. Numerous boat cruises that give expansive views of the surrounding peaks and quaint lakeside communities are available at the lake. Fans of water sports can engage in kayaking, windsurfing, and paddleboarding.

Lake Brienz

Nearby Attractions

- **Giessbach Falls:** The Giessbach Falls, one of Switzerland's most spectacular waterfall systems, flows into Lake Brienz after descending a number of stages. The magnificent Giessbach Hotel, where guests may savor fine meals and breathtaking vistas, is accessible via a vintage funicular railway, as are the falls.

Giessbach Falls

- **Brienz Rothorn Railway:** A nostalgic trip up to the summit of Brienzer Rothorn, with stunning views of the lake and surrounding mountains, is provided by this ancient steam railway. The trip itself is a highlight, providing a special means of taking in the natural splendor of the area.

Brienzer Rothorn Railway

Local Crafts and Culture

The centuries-old woodcarving history of the town of Brienz is well-known. Explore the galleries and studios in the area to see artists at work and buy locally made trinkets. The neighboring Ballenberg Open-Air Museum provides a fuller knowledge of the region's cultural past by showcasing traditional Swiss architecture and rural life.

Conclusion

Switzerland's undiscovered lakes and rivers combine natural beauty, recreational activities, and cultural diversity. These aquatic treasures provide life-changing experiences, whether you choose to explore the scenic and cultural attractions around Lake Brienz, swim in the azure waters of Caumasee, or simply unwind by the serene shores of Lake Oeschinen. Not only may visiting these lesser-known locations improve your vacation experience, but they also highlight Switzerland's genuine cultural and environmental richness.

Chapter Three: Charming Towns and Villages

The allure of Switzerland lies not only in its expansive vistas and vibrant metropolises, but also in its sleepy towns and villages that provide an insight into the nation's rich cultural heritage. This chapter explores three such magical locations, each with a distinct allure: Appenzell, Gruyères, and Murten.

Appenzell: Swiss Tradition Preserved

Traditional Architecture and Cultural Events

The charming town of Appenzell is located in northeastern Switzerland and is well known for its authentically maintained medieval Swiss architecture. The region is known for its wooden buildings with elaborate facades and vibrantly painted exteriors. The vibrant Landsgemeinde (open-air assembly) and the energetic Appenzell Folklore Festival, which features traditional music, dance, and costumes, are two of the town's most well-known cultural events.

Appenzell

Appenzell

Hiking and Nature Exploration

There are several hiking trails in the Appenzell region that are suitable for hikers of all skill levels. Hikes to Seealpsee and the Ebenalp offer breathtaking views of the Alpstein massif and a chance to take in the natural beauty of the area. The region is a nature lover's heaven since it is also home to a wide variety of plants and animals.

Local Cuisine and Crafts

The rich culinary legacy of Appenzell is another well-known feature. Specialties like Appenzeller cheese, which has a particular, powerful flavor, are part of the local cuisine. Explore the artisan stores and local markets to try and buy bread, cheese, and other traditional goods. The town is renowned for its artistry in carpentry and textiles, with numerous stores selling one-of-a-kind handcrafted goods.

Gruyères: Medieval Charm and Cheese

The Historic Castle and Town

Gruyères, a medieval village in the Fribourg canton, is well-known for its quaint alleys and exquisitely restored castle. Situated on a hill, the Château de Gruyères boasts a museum exhibiting the history and artistic creations of the surrounding landscape and provides panoramic views. Gruyères' charming stores, cafes, and restaurants line its cobblestone streets, evoking a mystical ambiance.

Gruyères

Gruyère Cheese Experience

Cheese is connected with Gruyères, especially the renowned Gruyère cheese. A local cheese factory called La Maison du Gruyère welcomes visitors to take a tour, taste a variety of aged cheeses, and learn about the process of creating cheese. In order to foster a deeper understanding of this culinary craft, the town frequently holds cheese-tasting events and workshops.

Museums and Art Galleries

Gruyères is home to the HR Giger Museum, which is devoted to the artwork of the Swiss artist renowned for his surreal and science fiction-inspired sculptures, in addition to the castle museum. The town is a center of the arts for the area, with a number of galleries and shows highlighting modern and local artists.

Murten: A Medieval Lakeside Town

Historical Significance and Attractions

Situated on Lake Murten, Murten is a town rich in its past. Due to the impressive preservation of the town's medieval walls and towers, tourists are able to stroll along the ramparts and take in views of the surrounding countryside and lake. There are many old buildings, quaint arcades, and lively squares in the Old Town, all of which tell a different tale about the town's history.

Murten

Local Festivals and Events

Murten's rich cultural legacy is showcased by the numerous festivals and activities held there all year long. The Murten Classics music festival honors classical music with performances in breathtaking historical settings, while the January Murten Light Festival turns the town into a riot of color and light. These occasions provide guests one-of-a-kind experiences that combine entertainment and culture.

Murten

Water Activities and Outdoor Adventures

The town is the perfect place for water sports including swimming, sailing, and paddleboarding because it is situated on the beaches of Lake Murten. The serene waters and picturesque surrounds of the lake provide an ideal environment for unwinding and having fun. There are also lots of bike and hiking routes in the vicinity of Murten, which offers further chances for outdoor exploration.

Conclusion

Switzerland's little cities and villages provide a singular fusion of culture, history, and scenic beauty. Every location offers a unique experience, from the historical significance and lakeside activities of Murten to the medieval charm and cheese heritage of Gruyères, the traditional architecture and cultural events of Appenzell, and more. Discovering these undiscovered treasures not only improves the quality of travel but also highlights the richness and diversity of Swiss customs and culture.

Chapter Four: Cultural and Historical Treasures

Grand abbeys, magnificent castles, and historic priories are just a few of the many structures that make up Switzerland's rich cultural and historical tapestry. This chapter explores three of Switzerland's greatest historical and cultural treasures: the Priory of Romainmôtier, the Abbey of Saint Gall, and Bellinzona's Castles. Each of these sites provides insightful information on the history and cultural legacy of the nation.

The Abbey of Saint Gall

Architectural Beauty and Historical Importance

One of the most important historical sites in Switzerland is the Abbey of Saint Gall, which is situated in the town of St. Gallen. The abbey, which dates back to the eighth century, was a significant hub of study and culture in the Middle Ages. Its magnificent Baroque building, complete with intricate frescoes and stucco, is a testament to its historical significance. The twin towers of the abbey church make it a magnificent example of ecclesiastical architecture.

Abbey of Saint Gall

The Library and Its Treasures

The library of the abbey is one of its most valuable possessions; it is regarded as one of the most exquisite and historic monastery libraries worldwide. More than 160,000 volumes, including rare manuscripts, early printed books, and incunabula, are kept in the library. The library's charm is enhanced by the interior's Rococo-style ceiling frescoes and elaborate woodwork. Viewers can discover the abbey's contribution to knowledge preservation over the ages by learning about these historical artifacts.

Abbey Library of Saint Gall

Visitor Information and Tips

All year long, the Abbey of Saint Gall is accessible to tourists. There are guided tours that provide detailed explanations of the history and architecture of the abbey. For information about special events and exhibitions, as well as opening hours, it is recommended to visit the abbey's official website. In order to protect the fragile manuscripts, photography is typically prohibited within libraries, thus patrons should make appropriate arrangements.

Bellinzona's Castles

Overview of the Three Castles

Three stunning medieval castles may be seen in Bellinzona, the capital of the Ticino canton: Castelgrande, Montebello, and Sasso Corbaro. These castles were part of a defensive system that kept the area safe from invaders. They were placed strategically on hillsides overlooking the town. Their historical significance is demonstrated by their magnificent battlements, towers, and walls.

Castelgrande

Montebello

Sasso Corbaro

Historical Significance and UNESCO Status

The Bellinzona castles have been inducted into the UNESCO World Heritage list due to their recognition of historical and cultural significance. They provide insights into the stormy history of the area and are a remarkable example of medieval military architecture. Control over the Alpine passes and the power battles between the Swiss Confederates and the Dukes of Milan were greatly aided by the castles.

Castle of Bellinzona

Exploring the Castles and Surrounding Area

The three castles can be independently explored by visitors, or they can take a trail connecting them all to get a thorough overview of the fortifications. Every castle has a museum with displays and relics pertaining to the history of the area. The experience is enhanced by the surroundings, which include the old town center and gorgeous scenery. The Medieval Days and the Bellinzona Wine Festival are two noteworthy occasions that highlight the history and culture of the region.

Romainmôtier Priory

Historical and Architectural Highlights

Nestled in the village of Romainmôtier-Envy, Romainmôtier Priory is one of Switzerland's oldest monasteries, having been established in the fifth century.

Constructed throughout the 10th and 12th centuries, the present-day Romanesque church is a magnificent example of medieval architecture. The priory's imposing yet austere architecture honors its role as a hub of pilgrimage and spirituality throughout history.

Romainmôtier Priory

Visiting the Priory and Nearby Attractions

The priory provides a calm and reflective setting and is open to visitors year-round. The church's interior is graced with stunning choir carvings, frescoes, and brickwork. The picturesque Jura Mountains are perfect for trekking and nature hikes, and the Maison de l'Absinthe in the commune of Môtiers provides information about the history and manufacture of absinthe.

Cultural Events and Festivals

The year-round cultural events and festivals held at Romainmôtier Priory improve the experience of visitors. The church's outstanding acoustics are used to present both classical and modern music at the yearly Music Festival of Romainmôtier. Medieval fairs, art shows, and themed tours showcasing the priory's historical and cultural legacy are among the other activities.

Conclusion

Discovering Switzerland's historical and cultural gems offers a deep appreciation of the nation's rich legacy. The impressive castles of Bellinzona, the historic Romainmôtier Priory, and the Abbey of Saint Gall, with its magnificent architecture and priceless library, all provide distinctive windows into Switzerland's history. Traveling to these locations enhances the experience of travel and emphasizes how crucial it is to protect these historical monuments for upcoming generations.

Chapter Five: Natural Wonders

Beautiful natural beauties decorate Switzerland's landscapes, captivating the senses and beckoning investigation. Three of the most amazing natural landmarks in the nation are highlighted in this chapter: the Rhine Falls, the Emosson Dam and Dinosaur Tracks, and the Creux du Van. Every location provides chances for outdoor recreation, historical significance, and distinctive geological features.

The Creux du Van

Geological Formation and Natural Beauty

Known as Switzerland's "Grand Canyon," the Creux du Van is a breathtaking natural amphitheater situated in the Jura Mountains. This amazing rock structure, which was formed by the erosion of limestone over millions of years, has 160-meter-high sheer cliffs that form a stunning semi-circular basin. Both scientists and anyone who enjoy the outdoors will find the landscape's expansive views and distinctive geological composition fascinating.

Creux du Van

Hiking and Wildlife Spotting

For lovers of the great outdoors and wildlife, the region surrounding the Creux du Van is a haven. A number of clearly designated paths take hikers through verdant woodlands and mountain meadows to the brink of the cliffs, offering chances to observe indigenous fauna like chamois, ibex, and a variety of bird species. The most well-liked hiking path is the four-hour loop trail from Noiraigue, which offers a moderately strenuous hike with scenic views.

Best Times to Visit

The late spring, summer, and early fall (May to October) seasons are ideal for visiting the Creux du Van because of the pleasant weather and accessibility of the trails. These seasons' abundant vegetation and blooming wildflowers accentuate the landscape's natural beauty, making them perfect for trekking and photography.

The Emosson Dam and Dinosaur Tracks

Engineering Marvel and Historical Site

In addition to being a remarkable engineering achievement, the Emosson Dam in the canton of Valais is also a location of great paleontological significance. The 180-meter-tall dam, which created the Lac d'Emosson reservoir, was finished in 1974. The region is well known for the finding of exceptionally well-preserved dinosaur footprints, which provide insight into the prehistoric past and are thought to be approximately 250 million years old.

Emosson Dam

Guided Tours and Outdoor Activities

There are guided tours available at the Emosson Dam that provide information about the building and maintenance of the structure as well as the paleontological significance of the dinosaur footprints. Other well-liked outdoor pursuits in the area include hiking, mountain biking, and paragliding. The popular walk to the dinosaur tracks combines the excitement of finding ancient footprints with a moderate hike.

Access and Transportation

There is parking close to the Emosson Dam, making it accessible by automobile. Alternatively, guests can travel from Martigny to the village of Le Châtelard on the picturesque Mont-Blanc Express train. From there, they can ascend a sequence of funiculars and board a panoramic train to reach the dam. Beautiful views of the neighboring valleys and the Mont Blanc Massif can be seen during this excursion.

The Rhine Falls

Europe's Largest Waterfall

The largest waterfall in Europe is the Rhine Falls, which are close to the town of Schaffhausen. The falls, which have a width of 150 meters and a height of 23 meters, are a stunning example of the might of nature. The water flow can approach 600,000 liters per second in the summer, producing a beautiful mist and a loud boom that enhance the dramatic picture.

Rhine Falls

Boat Tours and Viewing Platforms

Through boat cruises that navigate the choppy waters, visitors may get up close and personal with the Rhine Falls, providing a unique perspective of the falls. There are numerous viewing platforms thoughtfully positioned all around the falls, offering stunning vistas and fantastic photo ops. The most well-liked platform, which provides a comprehensive view of the falls' power, is perched atop Castle Rock and is reachable after a brief boat trip.

Nearby Attractions and Visitor Amenities

There are plenty of visitor amenities in the Rhine Falls region, such as dining options, gift stores, and spaces for picnics. The medieval castle Schloss Laufen, which is positioned above the falls and has a museum and guided tours, is one of the nearby attractions. A visit to Schaffhausen is also recommended since it offers the ideal fusion of natural beauty and cultural legacy with its quaint old town and the Munot stronghold.

Conclusion

The compelling variety of landscapes and sensations that Switzerland's natural beauties offer enhance the traveler's experience. The breathtaking power of the Rhine Falls, the towering cliffs of the Creux du Van, and the Emosson Dam's combination of engineering and prehistoric history all offer distinctive perspectives on Switzerland's natural beauty and geological diversity. Discovering these natural areas increases our awareness for the environment and emphasizes how crucial it is to protect these amazing landscapes for coming generations.

Chapter Six: Off the Beaten Path

Beyond the well-traveled routes lie Switzerland's hidden jewels, beckoning visitors to explore secluded valleys, tranquil scenery, and cultural treasures. Three off-the-beaten-path locations are examined in this chapter: the Lavaux Vineyards, the Bregaglia Valley, and Val Mustair. These areas provide a wonderful balance of historical significance, natural beauty, and cultural diversity, which makes them ideal for travelers looking for uncommon and immersive experiences.

Val Mustair: A Remote Alpine Valley

Monastery of St. John (UNESCO World Heritage)

Situated in the tranquil Val Mustair, the Monastery of St. John is a UNESCO World Heritage site renowned for its breathtaking murals and amazing Carolingian architecture. This Benedictine monastery was established by Charlemagne in the eighth century, and it has remained significant historically and spiritually down the ages. Explore the magnificent collection of religious items and medieval art in the museum, cloisters, and well-preserved chapel.

Monastery of St. John

Hiking and Nature Exploration

There are lots of hiking and natural exploration opportunities at Val Mustair. The immaculate scenery of the valley is interspersed with clearly signposted hiking routes suitable for every skill level. The area offers amazing views of the surrounding peaks and verdant valleys, whether taking leisurely strolls through alpine meadows or embarking on strenuous mountain climbs. The UNESCO-recognized Val Mustair Biosphere Reserve is a haven for environment lovers, with a wide variety of plants and fauna.

Val Mustair

Local Culture and Traditions

Local customs and culture are deeply ingrained in the Val Mustair region. Experience the distinctive Romansh language, folk music, and dances that honor the valley's rich history. A taste of the robust cultural life of the valley can be had at local festivals and events like the Chalandamarz spring festival. In addition, visitors may enjoy traditional Swiss cuisine in nearby restaurants and inns, where food is made with locally sourced, fresh ingredients.

The Bregaglia Valley

Scenic Beauty and Outdoor Activities

Southeast Switzerland's Bregaglia Valley is well known for its breathtakingly beautiful surroundings. Adventurers seeking a tranquil getaway will find solace in the valley's striking scenery, which includes untamed mountains, profound canyons, and charming towns. With many paths offering breathtaking views of the surrounding peaks and valleys, hiking, climbing, and mountain biking are popular outdoor pursuits.

Historical Villages and Architecture

Numerous medieval villages with well-maintained architecture and a rich cultural legacy can be found in the Bregaglia Valley. Often regarded as one of Switzerland's most picturesque villages, Soglio is home to the ancient Palazzo Salis, quaint stone homes, and winding lanes. Explore historic stone bridges, charming chapels, and old churches that showcase the architectural legacy of the valley.

Bregaglia Valley

Cultural Highlights

Highlights of the Bregaglia Valley's culture include regional artisan practices and artwork. The valley is rich in artistic history because it gave birth to the well-known painter Giovanni Segantini. Art lovers should not miss the Segantini Museum in St. Moritz, which is devoted to his creations. In addition, handcrafted goods such as textiles and wood carvings are manufactured by local artisans and sold in village stores and marketplaces.

The Lavaux Vineyards

Terraced Vineyards and Wine Tasting

The Lavaux Vineyards, which offer some of Switzerland's most breathtaking scenery, are situated along the northern shores of Lake Geneva and are recognized as a UNESCO World Heritage site. Some of the best wines in Switzerland are produced from the carefully maintained Roman-era terraced vineyards. Visitors can take part in wine tastings, take guided excursions around the vineyards, and discover more about the customs surrounding winemaking in the area.

Lavaux Vineyards

Scenic Walks and Cycling Routes

Numerous beautiful walking and cycling trails wind through the Lavaux region, offering breathtaking views of the surrounding vineyards, Lake Geneva, and the far-off Alps. A well-liked trail that passes by historic wine cellars, through quaint villages, and up the terraced hills is the Lavaux Vineyard Trail. Cycling lovers can explore the area on designated bike routes that meander through the lakefront vineyards.

UNESCO World Heritage Status

Numerous beautiful walking and cycling trails wind through the Lavaux region, offering breathtaking views of the surrounding vineyards, Lake Geneva, and the far-off Alps. A well-liked trail that passes by historic wine cellars, through quaint villages, and up the terraced hills is the Lavaux Vineyard Trail. Cycling lovers can explore the area on designated bike routes that meander through the lakefront vineyards.

Conclusion

Discovering Switzerland's lesser-known locations provides a fulfilling and interesting vacation experience. The picturesque scenery and historic villages of the Bregaglia Valley, the terraced slopes and winemaking traditions of the Lavaux Vineyards, and the distant alpine beauty and cultural legacy of Val Mustair all offer distinctive perspectives on the nation's varied and enthralling areas. These undiscovered beauties entice tourists to explore Switzerland's genuine and lesser-known treasures by going beyond the well-known.

Chapter Seven: Adventure and Outdoor Activities

With a plethora of outdoor activities to satisfy both thrill-seekers and nature lovers, Switzerland is a haven for adventure seekers. This chapter explores some of the most thrilling activities available in the nation, such as winter sports in Engelberg, paragliding in Interlaken, and Via Ferrata routes.

Via Ferrata Routes

Overview of Popular Routes

Climbers can securely cross otherwise impassable paths by using the Via Ferrata, sometimes known as the "iron path," which is a mountain route furnished with permanent ladders, ropes, and bridges. There are many Via Ferrata paths in Switzerland, and each one offers a different combination of natural beauty and difficulty. Well-traveled paths consist of:

- **Via Ferrata Kandersteg-Allmenalp:** Known for its stunning waterfalls and panoramic views.

Via Ferrata Kandersteg-Allmenalp

- **Via Ferrata Tälli:** One of the oldest routes, offering breathtaking alpine scenery.

Via Ferrata Tälli

- **Via Ferrata Murren-Gimmelwald:** Provides spectacular views of the Lauterbrunnen Valley and the Eiger, Mönch, and Jungfrau peaks.

Via Ferrata Murren-Gimmelwald

Safety Tips and Equipment

When traveling via Via Ferrata routes, safety must always come first. A Via Ferrata lanyard with energy absorbers, a harness, and a helmet are essential pieces of gear. Before leaving, it is imperative to examine the weather forecast and the state of the route. For their first experience, beginners may think about hiring a guide to ensure safety and good technique.

Best Times to Explore

The summer months of June through September are ideal for exploring Via Ferrata routes in Switzerland since the weather is more consistent and the trails are free of snow. An excellent time to visit is early autumn, when there are less tourists and beautiful fall foliage.

Paragliding in Interlaken

Overview of the Activity

Interlaken paragliding is an exhilarating way to take in the Swiss Alps from above. Renowned as one of the world's top paragliding locations, Interlaken offers amazing aerial views of the surrounding mountains and lakes Thun and Brienz.

Safety and Booking Information

In Interlaken, paragliding operators put safety first. Experienced pilots and tandem flights for novices guarantee a fun and safe flying experience. You can make reservations through any of the Interlaken adventure sports firms; the majority provide packages that include transportation to the launch location, rental gear, and the actual flight.

Scenic Routes and Experiences

The flights usually take off from Harder Kulm or Beatenberg and descend gently over the breathtaking scenery. Though the flight over the Swiss Alps only lasts for around twenty minutes, the memories made of it will last a lifetime. As mementos, you can typically buy pictures and films of the trip.

Winter Sports in Engelberg

Skiing and Snowboarding Options

Offering a range of skiing and snowboarding possibilities for all ability levels, Engelberg is one of Switzerland's top winter sports locations. Key areas include:

- **Titlis Glacier:** Known for its year-round skiing and the famous Titlis Rotair, the world's first rotating cable car.

Titlis Glacier

- **Jochpass and Trübsee:** Ideal for intermediate skiers and snowboarders, with a range of slopes and off-piste areas.

Jochpass and Trübsee

- **Brunni:** Perfect for families and beginners, featuring gentle slopes and a dedicated children's area.

Brunni

Other Winter Activities (Snowshoeing, Sledding)

Other wintertime activities available in Engelberg include sledding and snowshoeing. There are clearly signposted snowshoeing trails that lead through peaceful winter scenery. Fun for all ages, the Brunni toboggan run is a great place for sledding fans.

Accommodation and Dining

There are many different lodging options in Engelberg, ranging from luxurious hotels to quaint chalets and affordable hostels. Ski-in/ski-out access is provided by several locations, making it simple to go to the slopes every day. There is no shortage of dining alternatives, with foreign restaurants and après-ski bars alongside traditional Swiss restaurants providing hearty alpine food.

Conclusion

From the excitement of paragliding in Interlaken to the winter splendor of Engelberg, Switzerland's outdoor and adventure sports have something to offer everyone. In addition to giving guests a surge of adrenaline, these activities let them fully appreciate the breathtaking natural splendor of the Swiss Alps. Switzerland's undiscovered treasures await investigation by all skill levels of travelers, offering stunning scenery and life-changing experiences.

Chapter Eight: Relaxation and Wellness

Switzerland is well known for its amazing outdoor adventures and stunning scenery, but it's also a top location for rest and leisure. This chapter explores some of the best thermal springs, spas, and tranquil areas in the nation that are ideal for relaxation and revitalization.

Thermal Baths in Leukerbad

Overview of Thermal Spa Facilities

One of Europe's biggest thermal spa complexes is located in Leukerbad. The Leukerbad Therme and the Walliser Alpentherme & Spa, two of the village's many thermal bath facilities, use the naturally warm, mineral-rich waters to offer a variety of therapeutic treatments.

Leukerbad Therme

Walliser Alpentherme & Spa

Wellness Treatments and Services

Spa therapies available to guests include mineral massages, mud baths, and hydrotherapy. With a variety of indoor and outdoor pools that range in temperature from warm to hot, the thermal baths offer a relaxing experience amidst breathtaking alpine landscape.

Tips for a Relaxing Visit

To make the most of your visit to Leukerbad's thermal baths:

- Book treatments in advance to secure your preferred time slots.
- Visit during weekdays or early mornings to avoid crowds.
- Hydrate well before and after using the thermal waters.
- Take advantage of relaxation areas to unwind between treatments.

Bad Ragaz: Health and Wellness Retreat

Spa Facilities and Treatments

Reputable for its high-end spa services and wellness programs is Bad Ragaz. Along with a range of thermal pools, steam rooms, and saunas, the Tamina Therme also provides holistic health services, massages, and cosmetic therapies.

Bad Ragaz

Tamina Therme

Outdoor Activities and Scenic Beauty

Bad Ragaz offers a plethora of outdoor activities in addition to its spa. Discover the picturesque Tamina Gorge, play golf on immaculate courses, or take leisurely strolls through the immaculate parks and gardens are all available to visitors.

Cultural and Culinary Experiences

In addition to fitness, Bad Ragaz provides a wealth of culinary and cultural attractions. The town is home to music festivals and art exhibits, and its restaurants offer gourmet fare with an emphasis on locally grown, fresh ingredients.

The Quiet Beauty of the Emmental Region

Scenic Landscapes and Tranquility

The Emmental region is known for its beautiful scenery and serene surroundings. The tranquil surroundings of lush meadows, quaint villages, and rolling hills are ideal for unwinding. For people wishing to get away from the rush of modern life, this picturesque location is perfect.

Local Cheese Dairies and Gastronomy

Emmental is well-known for its cheese, so it's imperative to visit the nearby dairies. In addition to tasting a range of cheeses, including the well-known Emmental cheese, visitors may learn about the traditional methods used to make cheese. There are restaurants in the area that serve hearty Swiss dishes produced with local, fresh ingredients, and the food is great as well.

Walking and Cycling Routes

Many walking and cycling trails wind through the picturesque surroundings of the Emmental region. These routes range in difficulty from kid-friendly, leisurely paths to more strenuous courses for serious hikers and cyclists. The clearly designated pathways offer an ideal means of leisurely exploring the area's scenic splendor.

Conclusion

Switzerland's wellness and leisure hidden jewels provide the ideal counterpoint to the nation's more daring attractions. These locations offer the perfect environments for relaxing and recharging, from the serene beauty of the Emmental region to the sophisticated spa retreats of Bad Ragaz and the restorative thermal baths of Leukerbad. Seize the chance to unwind and lose yourself in the tranquil and healing settings that Switzerland has to offer.

Conclusion

Summary of Switzerland's Hidden Gems

As we come to the end of "Switzerland's Hidden Gems: Discovering Distinctive Tourism Destinations," it's evident that the country has much more to offer than just its popular tourist attractions. This tour unveils a plethora of lesser-known locations that highlight Switzerland's varied beauty and rich legacy, from the Alps to the tranquil hidden lakes, from quaint towns and villages to cultural and historical treasures, and from natural wonders to spa retreats.

Recap of Key Destinations and Highlights

We have explored the historical charm of Appenzell and Gruyères, marveled at the tranquil beauty of Lake Oeschinen and Caumasee, and journeyed into the alpine wonderlands of Zermatt and Saas-Fee. We marveled at the natural wonders of the Creux du Van and the Rhine Falls, as well as the architectural grandeur of the Abbey of Saint Gall and the ancient Bellinzona fortresses. We also experienced the peace of Val Mustair, the picturesque charm of the Bregaglia Valley, and the healing spa treatments in Leukerbad and Bad Ragaz.

Encouragement to Explore Further

Discovering Switzerland's undiscovered treasures is highly recommended, as each one provides an exceptional experience that goes beyond the conventional travel schedule. These locations promise life-changing experiences and lasting memories as they entice you to explore Switzerland's landscapes, history, and culture in greater detail.

Inspiring Readers to Discover More of Switzerland

Let your journey through Switzerland begin with this guide. There are a gazillion more undiscovered beauties, each with a unique charm and tale. Switzerland offers plenty to offer everyone, regardless of their interests—hiking enthusiasts, history buffs, or those looking for some quiet time to themselves. To fully appreciate the complexity and diversity of this stunning land, embrace the spirit of exploration and go off the usual route.

Final Thoughts

The process of writing this book has been one of wonder and appreciation for Switzerland's undiscovered beauties. Every location that is featured in this guide is proof of the nation's diverse array of historical significance, natural beauty, and cultural riches. We hope that reading this book has piqued your interest in visiting these amazing locations.

Reflection on the Journey

It's clear from looking back on this tour of Switzerland's hidden gems that these locations provide more than just beautiful scenery and insightful historical information. They create a stronger bond between the land and its inhabitants and increase respect for Switzerland's distinct identity. Discovering these undiscovered treasures has served as a poignant reminder of the value of pursuing and valuing the lesser-known regions of the globe.

Importance of Sustainable and Respectful Tourism

Finally, keep in mind the significance of courteous and sustainable tourism as you go out on your adventures. These undiscovered treasures are priceless and ought to be saved for next generations. Reduce your environmental footprint, respect local customs, and patronize neighborhood businesses. By doing this, you make sure that these stunning locations stay pristine and attract tourists for many years to come.

We appreciate you coming along as we discover some of Switzerland's best-kept secrets. I hope you have an amazing journey full of surprises, wonders, and lifelong memories.

Appendices

1. Glossary of Terms

- **Alpine**: Referring to the high mountains of the Alps, often used to describe the culture, flora, and fauna of the region.
- **UNESCO World Heritage Site**: A landmark or area recognized by the United Nations Educational, Scientific, and Cultural Organization for its cultural, historical, or scientific significance.
- **Via Ferrata**: A protected climbing route found in the Alps and certain other locations. It uses fixed cables, rungs, and bridges.
- **Thermal Baths**: Pools filled with naturally heated mineral water, known for their therapeutic properties.
- **Glacier**: A large, slow-moving mass of ice, found in the high mountain ranges and polar regions.
- **Medieval**: Relating to the Middle Ages, a period in European history from the 5th to the late 15th century.
- **Belle Époque**: A period characterized by peace, prosperity, and cultural advancements, typically dating from the late 19th century to the start of World War I.
- **Baroque**: An elaborate and highly detailed style of architecture, art, and music that originated in the early 17th century.
- **Cultural Heritage**: The legacy of physical artifacts and intangible attributes of a group or society inherited from past generations.
- **Sustainable Tourism**: Tourism that takes full account of its current and future economic, social, and environmental impacts, addressing the needs of visitors, the industry, the environment, and host communities.

2. Recommended Reading and Resources

- **Books**
    - o "Swiss Watching: Inside the Land of Milk and Money" by Diccon Bewes

o "Slow Train to Switzerland" by Diccon Bewes
o "Rick Steves Switzerland" by Rick Steves
o "Switzerland's Mountain Inns: A Walking Vacation in a World Apart" by Marcia and Philip Lieberman
o "Swiss Made: The Untold Story Behind Switzerland's Success" by James Breiding

- **Websites**
  o Switzerland Tourism
  o Swiss UNESCO World Heritage Sites
  o Swiss Federal Office of Culture
  o Swiss National Park
  o MySwitzerland.com - Nature & Parks
- **Documentaries**
  o "Wild Switzerland" (BBC)
  o "Switzerland from Above" (National Geographic)
  o "The Alps: The High Life" (PBS Nature)

3. Maps of Key Destinations

Note: Maps are typically visual, but the descriptions below guide you on what to include in each map.

- **Map 1: The Enchanting Alps**
  o Zermatt and the Matterhorn
  o Saas-Fee
  o Lauterbrunnen Valley
  o Aletsch Glacier

Map of Zermatt and the Matterhorn

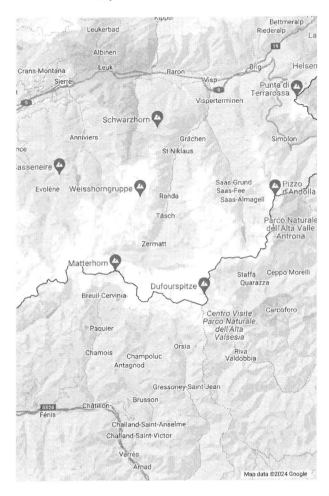

Map of Saas-Fee

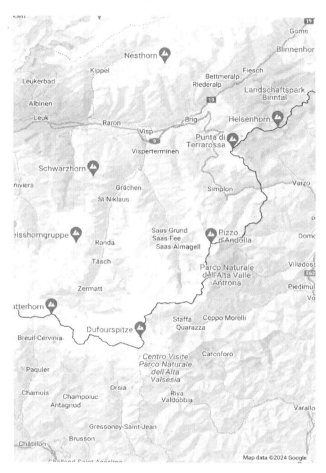

Map of Lauterbrunnen Valley

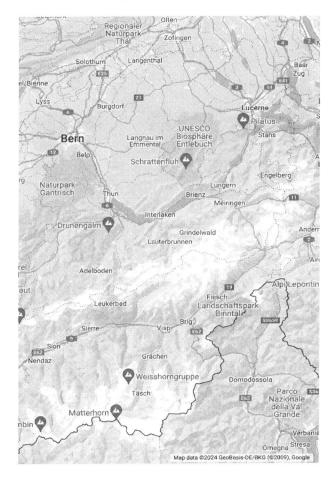

Map of Aletsch Glacier

Gross Grünhorn

Finste

Konkordiahütte SAC

Fiescher
Gabelhorn

Gross
Wannenhorn

eckhorn

Olmenhorn

Strahlhorn

Am Al

Map data ©2024 Google

- **Map 2: Hidden Lakes and Waterways**
  - o Lake Oeschinen
  - o Caumasee
  - o Lake Brienz

Map of Lake Oeschinen

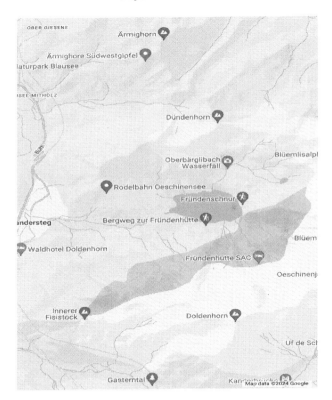

Map of Caumasee

Map of Lake Brienz

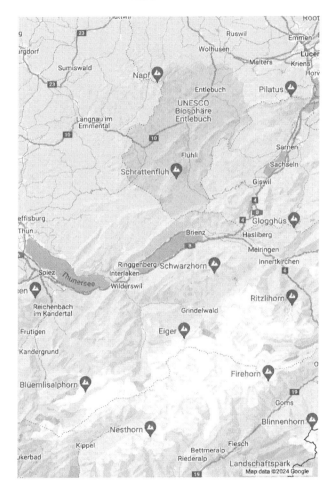

- **Map 3: Charming Towns and Villages**
  - o Appenzell
  - o Gruyères
  - o Murten

Map of Appenzell

Map of Gruyères

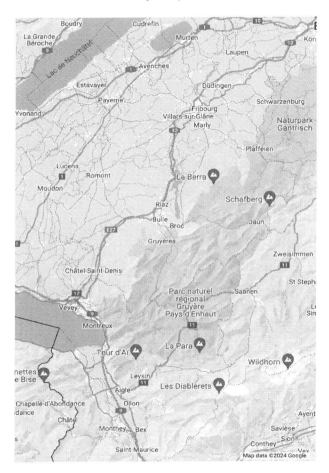

Map of Murten

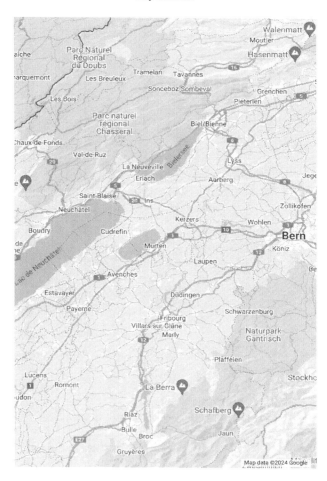

- **Map 4: Cultural and Historical Treasures**
  - o The Abbey of Saint Gall
  - o Bellinzona's Castles
  - o Romainmôtier Priory

Map of Abbey of Saint Gall

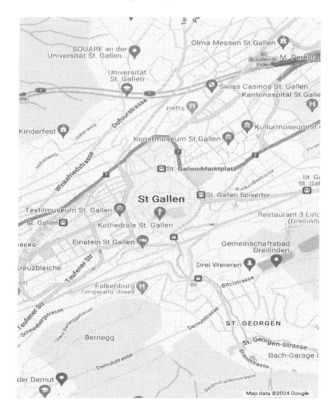

Bellinzona's Castles

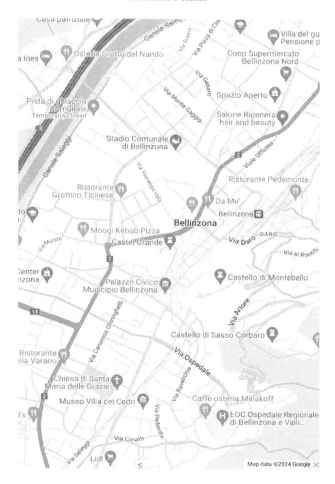

Romainmôtier Priory

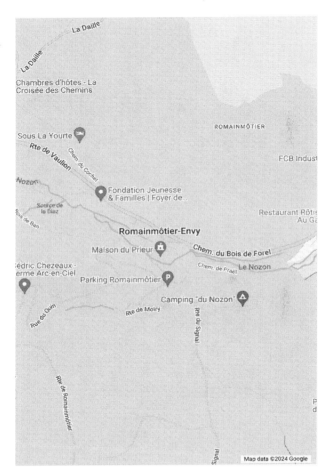

- **Map 5: Natural Wonders**
  - o   The Creux du Van
  - o   The Emosson Dam and Dinosaur Tracks
  - o   The Rhine Falls

Map of Creux du Van

Map of Emosson Dam and Dinosaur Tracks

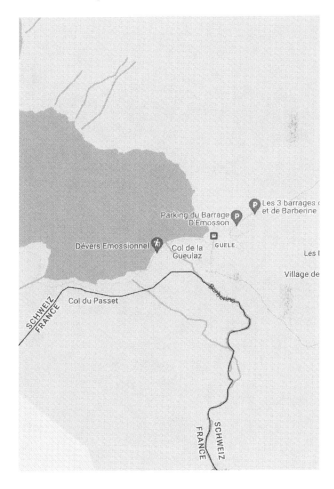

Map of Rhine Falls

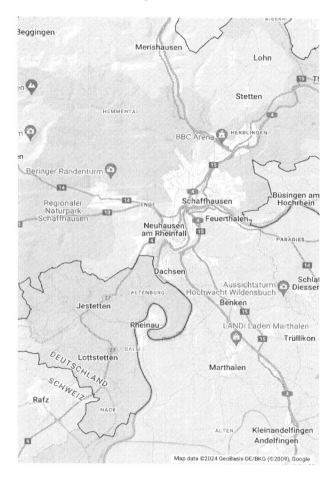

- **Map 6: Off the Beaten Path**
  - o Val Mustair
  - o The Bregaglia Valley
  - o The Lavaux Vineyards

Map of Val Mustair

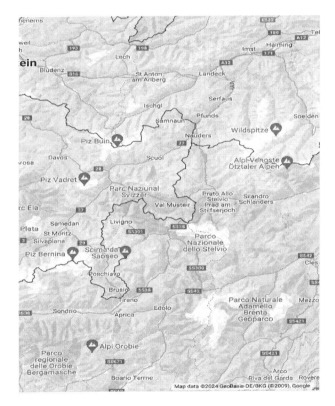

Map of Bregaglia Valley

Map of Lavaux Vineyards

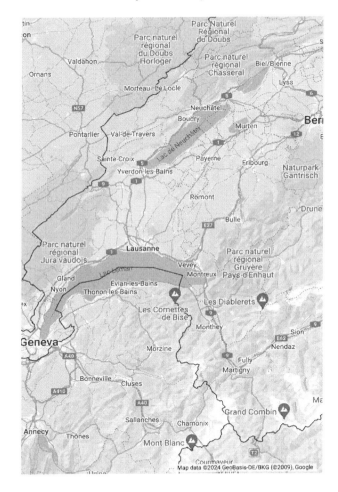

4. Contact Information for Tourist Offices and Guides

- **Switzerland Tourism**
  - o Website: MySwitzerland.com
  - o Phone: +41 44 288 11 11
  - o Email: info@switzerland.com
- **Zermatt Tourism**
  - o Website: Zermatt.ch
  - o Phone: +41 27 966 81 00
  - o Email: info@zermatt.ch
- **Gruyères Tourism**
  - o Website: La Gruyère Tourisme
  - o Phone: +41 848 424 424
  - o Email: info@la-gruyere.ch
- **Lauterbrunnen Tourism**
  - o Website: Lauterbrunnen Valley
  - o Phone: +41 33 856 85 68
  - o Email: info@lauterbrunnen.swiss
- **Bellinzona Tourism**
  - o Website: Bellinzona e Valli Turismo
  - o Phone: +41 91 825 21 31
  - o Email: info@bellinzonaevalli.ch
- **Lake Brienz Tourism**
  - o Website: Brienz Tourismus
  - o Phone: +41 33 952 80 80
  - o Email: info@brienz-tourismus.ch
- **Val Mustair Tourism**
  - o Website: Biosfera Val Müstair
  - o Phone: +41 81 851 60 60
  - o Email: info@val-muestair.ch
- **Lavaux Vineyards Tourism**
  - o Website: Lavaux Unesco

o   Phone: +41 21 946 27 70

o   Email: info@lavaux-unesco.ch

This appendices section is designed to be a comprehensive resource for readers, providing additional information and tools to enhance their exploration of Switzerland's hidden gems.

Index

- o Local crafts and culture
- o Nearby attractions (Giessbach Falls, Brienz Rothorn Railway)

C

- Caumasee: The Turquoise Jewel
  - o Best times to visit
  - o Surrounding flora and fauna
  - o Swimming and boating activities
- Creux du Van
  - o Best times to visit
  - o Geological formation and natural beauty
  - o Hiking and wildlife spotting

E

- Emmental Region, The Quiet Beauty of
  - o Local cheese dairies and gastronomy
  - o Scenic landscapes and tranquility
  - o Walking and cycling routes
- Emosson Dam and Dinosaur Tracks
  - o Access and transportation
  - o Engineering marvel and historical site
  - o Guided tours and outdoor activities
- Engelberg, Winter Sports in
  - o Accommodation and dining
  - o Other winter activities (snowshoeing, sledding)
  - o Skiing and snowboarding options

G

- Gruyères: Medieval Charm and Cheese
  - o Gruyère cheese experience

This index provides a comprehensive guide to the topics and destinations covered in "Switzerland's Hidden Gems: Discovering Distinctive Tourism Destinations," allowing readers to easily navigate and find specific information throughout the book.